The Underground Railroad

DISCOVER PICTURES AND FACTS ABOUT THE UNDERGROUND RAILROAD FOR KIDS!

This was one of the most important parts of the civil war, and it provided safe passage for African Americans to get to freedom and away from slavery. Here are the facts about it.

It was never a railroad, but it was actually safe houses and people who helped slaves escape to the north or to Canada.

The slaveholders and the law officials did look for these safe houses and people who helped them, trying to bring them back to the owners.

Slavery actually existed in the US before it was even a country, so it's been a problem for at least 100 years before the underground railroad was established.

Most who were involved in the system were members that were part of the free black community, such as church leaders, philanthropists, and also abolitionists.

The Quakers were also a big part of helping slaves since they believed it was wrong.

The safe house travel was done at night and on foot, and usually, if they were caught they were sent back to the owners.

If the conductors who helped the slaves were caught, they were at risk of hanging.

One of the most famous members of this was Harriet Tubman, who helped so many slaves escape to the north.

The railroad was actually a very informal network with many different routes, most going to the north, and later to Canada or to the Caribbean or Mexico.

The railroad language was actually a secret code that people used, and many times, coded sign language was used to communicate.

The underground Railroad was quite an interesting event, and it helped many get freedom back during this tumultuous time.

Printed in the USA
CPSIA information can be obtained
at www.ICGtesting.com
LVRC090820090923
757505LV00008B/126